Dune Buggies

By E. S. Budd

The Child's World®

Published by The Child's World®
PO Box 326
Chanhassen, MN 55317-0326
800-599-READ
www.childsworld.com

Design and Production:
The Creative Spark, San Juan Capistrano, CA

Photo Credits: Inset page 6 courtesy of Bruce and Winnie Myers.
All other images ©2003 David M. Budd Photography.

Library of Congress Cataloging-in-Publication Data
Cataloging-in-Publication data for this title has been applied for and is available
from the United States Library of Congress.

Contents

Let's Go Duning!　　　　　　4

Climb Aboard!　　　　　　20

Up Close　　　　　　22

Glossary　　　　　　24

Let's Go Duning!

Dune buggies are made for cruising on beaches, sand dunes, and other recreational areas. Duning is a great way for family and friends to spend time together.

These small vehicles have very powerful engines. An open **chassis** makes them lighter than other cars. This helps them go really fast. Dune buggies are awesome!

NEW CRAZE- OFF THE ROAD FUN CARS
BUILD YOUR OWN RUGGED ROD-$75 UP!

HOT ROD
EVERYBODY'S AUTOMOTIVE MAGAZINE

INDY '500' DAY BY
DAY DIARY! NHRA
SpringNationals

RING & PINION GEAR
SETTING MADE EASY!

SPECIAL SECTION ON DUNE BUGGIES,
4-WHEEL-DRIVE &
HOME-BUILT
CARS

In the 1950s, a man named Bruce Meyer built the first dune buggy. He saw people riding heavy, crude vehicles on the beach. It looked like fun. He knew a light car could move at higher speeds. That would be even more fun!

Meyers decided to build his own machine. He used the shortened frame of a Volkswagen. He added a **fiberglass** chassis. The result was the "Meyers Manx." This car was so cool, it was featured on the cover of magazines. Some of today's dune buggies (like the red one at left) look a lot like the old Meyers Manx.

Soon people wanted a fast, fun dune buggy for themselves. Meyers created kits so that people could build their own buggies. Some riders used Volkswagen Beetles like this one to build their own custom dune buggies.

Today dune buggies come in all shapes
and sizes.

They all have one thing in common:
they're a lot of fun to drive!

Dune buggies have big wheels and tires. The back tires have special treads called paddles that grip the sand. They keep the vehicles from getting stuck. The front tires are smooth. They glide across the sand to keep the buggy moving.

Duners know it's important to stay safe. They follow the recreation area's rules. They also use safety equipment. Duners often travel over rough terrain and perform daring tricks. **Roll cages** protect drivers and passengers if the vehicles roll over.

Special seatbelts with shoulder **harnesses** keep riders safely in the buggy. Duners wear goggles or glasses to protect their eyes. A flag is attached to a long, flexible rod called a whip. The flag keeps buggies visible as they move up and down the dunes.

For the best drivers, dune buggy drag racing is a lot of fun. Drivers race to see who has the fastest buggy. Safe drivers stay in control. Only the most experienced duners should go fast. It can be dangerous to drive too close to other vehicles.

Powerful engines make it easy for dune buggies to "pop a wheelie" or catch air—it's almost like flying!

Climb Aboard!

Would you like to see what it's like to go duning? Drivers use steering wheels to control their buggies. Instruments give the driver information. They show how much gas is in the tank or how fast the buggy is moving. Other instruments let the driver know how the engine is running. Dune buggies have pedals like those in a car. They operate the **brakes, clutch,** and **accelerator.**

1. Steering wheel

2. Instruments

3. Clutch

4. Brake

5. Accelerator

21

Up Close

Since dune buggies travel off-road, the ride can be very bumpy. Large **shock absorbers** make the ride more comfortable. A powerful engine is mounted on the back of the vehicle. Dune buggies have headlights so duners can drive at night.

1. Tires
2. Shock absorbers
3. Whip
4. Roll cage
5. Engine
6. Headlights

Glossary

accelerator (ak-SELL-ur-ay-tur) An accelerator controls the speed of a vehicle. A dune buggy has an accelerator pedal.

brakes (BRAYKS) Brakes are controls that help a driver stop or slow down. A dune buggy has a brake pedal.

chassis (CHA-see) A chassis is the outside frame of a vehicle. A dune buggy has an open chassis.

clutch (KLUTCH) A clutch is a control used to change gears on a vehicle. A dune buggy has a clutch pedal.

fiberglass (FY-bur-glass) Fiberglass is a strong, light material made of glass and plastic. Some dune buggies have a fiberglass chassis.

harnesses (HAR-nis-ez) Harnesses are sturdy straps. A dune buggy has seatbelts with shoulder harnesses that hold drivers and passengers in their seats.

roll cages (ROLL KAY-jez) Roll cages are a protective framework of metal bars on a vehicle. A dune buggy has a roll cage for safety.

shock absorbers (SHOCK ab-SOR-burz) Shock absorbers are springs between the wheels and the chassis of a vehicle. A dune buggy has large shock absorbers to make the ride more comfortable.